I0441677

GOVERNMENT AUCTIONS/SALES MANUAL

8th Edition

Published by
The McKee Company
P.O. Box 22996
Denver, CO 80222

www.themckeecompany.com

© Copyright 2000-2016 by Ellen L. Hughes

This book is licensed for your personal use only. This may not be re-sold or given away to others. If you would like to share this book with another person, please purchase an additional copy for each recipient. If you are reading this book and did not purchase it, or it was not purchased for your use only, then please return to your favorite book retailer and purchase your own copy.

TABLE OF CONTENTS

INTRODUCTION

This book, **_Government Auctions/Sales Manual (GASM)_** is designed to enhance and simplify your auction experience.

The Federal Government purchases more supplies and materials than any other entity in the world. As a result, they dispose opuf large amounts of excess and

surplus personal property each year, thus saving millions of taxpayer dollars by selling personal and real property to the general public.

Because there is no standard method set for these agencies to sell surplus and seized property, each one has devised their own unique system. It can be very time-consuming to locate and participate in the auctions that sell the type of property you want.

> *NOTE: You will find more government agencies are relying on the Internet to hold auctions.   If you do not have a home computer, most libraries have computers for your use.*

Follow the detailed instructions and you will be armed with information that should guarantee you success at auctions. Making intelligent and profitable decisions does not require a lot of work on your part, **_you just need the correct information_**.

Use **GASM** during every step of your auction experience. Highlight information important to you or something you may want to look at a little more in depth. There is a lot of information contained herein; do not try to memorize it. _Take GASM with you when you attend auctions or go comparison shopping._ We kept **GASM** this size so you can use it for quick reference any time.

Because there are so many participating agencies, the information (phone numbers, addresses, etc.) changes constantly. _Let us keep you informed of changes._ Subscribe to Quarterly Updates by filling out the form on Page 152. You will be kept up to date on the agencies listed herein.

Remember, if it sounds too good to be true, it usually is. There are a lot of so-called "experts" who will make it sound easy to find a good deal. Truth is, auctions are more widely publicized than ever. You need to be as knowledgeable as possible to find the good deals.

Now get ready to read a great book - _**Government Auctions/Sales Manual**_. The best tool you have to be profitable in the auction business!

⌘　⌘　⌘　⌘　⌘

BIDDER'S CHECKLIST

As you would with any business deal, you need to equip yourself with as much information as possible to make the correct decision. The more attention you pay to details before and during the sale, the smoother the transaction after the sale should you be the winning bidder.

Before the Sale

Read the Sales Catalog Completely. Information regarding sale items, date, time, location, removal and payment policies, plus other pertinent data, is in the pre-sale information packet. If there is no pre-sale information to review, call the contact person (where provided), auction house or government agency which is holding the auction. **Pay particular attention to removal policies.**

Research, Research, Research. After determining what type of property you are interested in, check the **current market value of it.** Be certain the item you are researching is the same item; check model number, style, size, weight and any distinguishing features. For more information on comparison shopping, see Page 17.

Inspect the Merchandise. Thoroughly inspect any item on which you intend to bid. The majority of items sold at auctions are used; additionally, there may be a disclaimer stating that no warranty is given, expressed or implied. Therefore, it is very important that you **carefully inspect merchandise before bidding on it.** If inspection occurs the same day as the auction, get there early to inspect the merchandise. For on-line auction or remote inspection information, see Page 8

Review the Terms of Sale and Conditions. They vary from sale to sale. Be sure you **understand each expression (terminology) used**. (See Page 146 for Glossary) If you have questions, call the contact number/person for further details.

Verify Unit and Total Price Before Completing a Bid. Know the unit type, (for example, lot versus each) and bid accordingly. Mistakes can prove costly and will delay processing your bid. **Initial all erasures and changes made on your bid.**

Verify Mailing Address With Address Listed in Sales Catalog. Some agencies hold more two or more sales *simultaneously* and different addresses will be listed for different sale sites. *Allow extra time for delivery when mailing a bid.*

Be Sure Your Bid is Responsive. Make sure your bid is submitted in the **proper unit of measure** (i.e., pound, foot, each, ton.

Have the Correct Form of Payment. **Form of payment differs from one agency to another**. For detailed information particular to a sale, check the *Terms of Sale* listed in the flyer or catalog.

At the Sale

Be Prompt. Last-minute **changes may be made** at the start of a sale, such as withdrawals or additions to the advertised terms or merchandise. <u>Bidders are bound by these announcements</u>. Be sure you are there on time to hear any such statements.

Take Picture I.D. A picture I.D. (such as driver's license or passport) **is necessary** to make purchases at almost every sale or auction.

Register to Bid. Your bidder number identifies you as the registered bidder and authorizes you to bid on any item of interest. **You are responsible for your bidder number** and the bid made with that number. Do not allow other persons to use your number; you will be held accountable.

Use the Correct Form. A common requirement is that **bids be submitted on specified forms**. These forms are included in the pre-sale information available.

Have Questions? When you register, ask the sales associates any questions you have regarding payment policy and removal of merchandise.

Pay Attention. Before bidding on any items make sure you can understand an auctioneer . Every auctioneer is different in his/her style and chant and you will be able to understand some auctioneers better than others. Don't bid if you can't figure out what the auctioneer is saying.

Don't Talk. **Be considerate**; don't talk during an indoor auction. It is hard enough to understand an auctioneer because they talk loud and fast. If you need to chat, go somewhere out of earshot of the other attendees. Bidders and auctioneers alike will benefit.

Know Which Lot is Being Sold. Bidding progresses very quickly. Pay attention to the bidding process and be sure of what you are bidding on and the amount of your bid. **Failure to pay attention** or bidder misunderstanding will not cancel a sale.

Note Which Lots Are "Export Only". There are no exceptions to these export requirements. Purchase wisely. "Export Only" means merchandise cannot remain in U.S. (See **Export Information** on Page 38).

Set Limits for Your Bid. Determine your maximum bid will be and abide by it. **Don't exceed it.**

Be Aware of Removal Condition. Don't bid for more material than you can afford and remove within the time allowed. **Failure to remove property** may result in forfeiture of any right, title and interest. The property may revert and repossess to the agency without further notice to buyer and will result in any monies paid being forfeited and the transaction shall be null and void.

Tax Exemption. Sales tax is usually collected at auctions. If you are exempt, **bring your tax certificate.**

Be Alert. Although it is illegal, there may be a few instances where you notice people bidding just to drive the bidding up. If you see someone who bids a lot but never buys anything, he may be a shill. This is a rare occurrence, but it can happen. Be aware of this and **make sure you aren't bidding against yourself**.

Buy Like You Are Going To Resell. When you decide to bid on an item, think about what you are going to pay for it and what you could get if you resold it. This approach may help you decide if the item is worth the price you are willing to pay for it.

After Making a Successful Bid

Payment Procedures. **Know when payment is due.** At

some sales, payment is due immediately upon completion of bidding. The bidder should proceed to a cashier to a Notice of Award (receipt for purchase and necessary to pick up merchandise). At other sales, there may be an extended period of time to make payment. The seller may, at its discretion, exceed the closing beyond this period to process liens, effect clear title or perform other legalities.

Know When Property Should Be Removed. Be sure to check the Terms of Sale of each sale for specific information regarding payment and removal. The Terms of Sale **provide removal dates and guide-lines** for both export and domestic goods.

Arrange for Removal of the Property. If removal must be made on the day of sale, **have transportation prearranged** for large or immobile objects.

On-Line Auctions

On-line auctions should be treated as auctions held in brick-and-mortar buildings, with a few extra precautions.

Precautions to take:

- Know exactly what you're bidding on. If you're not sure, e-mail the seller and ask specific questions.

- Pay by credit card. Most credit card issuers provide 100 percent on-line protection.

- If you win the bid, print out the photos, descriptions

and e-mails exchanged with the seller. Insure the item and pay promptly. Keep all records until the item is received and verified.

- If there are problems, first try to work it out with the seller. If a dispute can't be resolved, contact the credit card company and the auction site. If that doesn't work, file a report with the Federal Trade Commission.

- Decide how high you're willing to bid for the item and stick to it. This prevents heat-of-the-moment decisions especially in highly competitive bidding.

⌘ ⌘ ⌘ ⌘ ⌘

TYPE OF SALES/AUCTIONS

Absolute Auction - Property is sold to highest bidder with no limiting conditions or amount. The seller may not bid personally or through an agent. Also known as an auction without reserve.

Auction - A method of selling in a public forum through open and competitive bidding. Also referred to as public auction, auction sale or sale.

Auction With Reserve - The seller or agent reserves the right to accept or decline any and all bids. A minimum acceptable price may or may not be disclosed and the seller reserves the right to accept or decline any bid within a specified time.

Candle Auction - Phone mail is the method of bidding. A minimum bid or asking price will be established and prospective bidders will be required to place a deposit in order to participate.

Cash and Carry - Sales that offer small quantities of items at fixed prices based on current market value.

Consignment Sale - Sale of merchandise consigned to a local auction house when it is not cost-effective to transport it to a sales center.

Cyclic Sale - Public auction held on a regular basis.

Fixed-Price Sale - The selling prices are posted on the property and items are sold on a first-come basis.

Negotiated/Quick Sale - Sale of merchandise by negotiation or best offer. Bids are made before you attend the auction. Sales are usually used for low-dollar value sales or perishable goods.

On-Line Auction - An auction that accepts bids via the Internet; usually through the Web-based form, but occasionally via e-mail.

Open Bid Sale - Bidders write their offer on a publicly-posted bid form. This is used for property whose quantity, location or value does not merit relocation to a sale center.

Portfolio Sale - Sale comprised of a combination of real properties and then broken into several pools. These pools are then sold individually.

Sealed Bid Sale - Utilized where confidential bids are submitted to be opened at a predetermined place and time, usually of geographically-isolated merchandise. Not a true auction in that it does not allow for reaction from the competitive market place.

Specialty/Ad Hoc Sale - A public auction scheduled on an as-needed basis when the volume or the unique nature and dollar value justifies such a sale.

Spot Bid - A variation on the sealed bid. Instead of opening the bids, the auctioneers invites others to bid in a public sale. Once all the bids are in, they are compared and the highest bid takes the property.

⌘   ⌘   ⌘   ⌘   ⌘

LETTER OF CREDIT

A Letter of Credit (L/C) is a document consisting of specific instructions by a buyer of goods, that is issued by a bank, to the seller who is authorized to draw a specified amount of money from the issuing bank, its branches, or other associate banks or agencies under certain conditions, i.e., the receipt by the bank of certain documents within a given time.

It may be revocable or irrevocable. An irrevocable L/C provides a guarantee by the issuing bank in the event that all terms and conditions are met by the buyer (or drawee). A revocable L/C can be canceled or altered by the drawee after it has been issued by drawee's bank. A confirmed L/C is one issued by a foreign bank which is validated or guaranteed by a U.S. bank for a U.S. exporter in the case of default by the foreign buyer or bank.

Because the amount, date and agency name are included in the letter, **a separate Letter of Credit must be obtained for each sale**. Some banks charge for this service.

A Letter of Credit is written on the financial institution's letterhead.

⌘　⌘　⌘　⌘　⌘

COMPARISON SHOPPING/BUYERS

As stated previously in the Bidders Checklist (Page 7), researching the property you are interested in is the most important step you should take. Unless you are an expert in a particular field, it is imperative to determine the fair market value of an item before you can determine your bidding limit.

There are several ways to do this. One of the easiest and fastest ways is to check the Internet. Using one of the browsers, type in the type of property you are researching. If you have the manufacturer's name, include it. If you don't have a home computer, you can always go to the library.

Another place to check when comparison shopping is the classified advertising section of the local newspaper. Find similar items in the classifieds that are being offered and check their prices. Make sure the items are similar in as many ways possible: year, condition, etc. Now you will have a range with which to set your bid limit.

Consult with a *professional*. For items like antiques and fine art, check with local dealers or reference books. Ask the dealers their opinions on certain items, what's hot and what's not selling. Consult with professional for any type of property. Ask about outdated and discontinued equipment, such as computers and office equipment.

Pawnbrokers can also be an excellent source. Talk to them and find out what items sell well. If an item is not selling, avoid bidding on these items unless you already have a buyer.

Contact businesses in the ***Yellow Pages*** that deal in the particular goods you are wanting to purchase, (i.e. Used Office Equipment, Construction Equipment, Scrap Metals Recycling, Restaurant Equipment, Used Automobiles, etc.)

While you are at the library check out professional trade journals that carry specifics for the latest developments in a particular industry, (i.e., electronics). From these you can determine what item is valuable and what is ready for the trash.

Buyers

Some people sell the property they purchase at auctions. Use the following sources to locate buyers for your surplus merchandise.

Books:

<u>American Wholesalers and Distributors Directory</u>
Published by Gale Research Inc.

A comprehensive guide offering industry details on approximately 27,000 wholesalers and distributors of consumer products in the U. S.

Entries include:
-Name/address/telephone/FAX/telex numbers
-Standard Industrial Classification (SIC) Codes
-Annual estimated sales for most companies
-Principal product lines
-Key personnel/Number of employees
-Financial information

Other features include statistical profiles and snapshots showing historical activity; uniform industry and product statistics for up to 590 MSAs; and industry and labor force statistics by state.

Information is listed:

-Alphabetically by company name
-Geographically by state and city
-According to Standard Industrial Classification Codes

Million Dollar Directory

This directory includes background information on all businesses in the U.S. and Canada with business profiles on firms in over 200 countries worldwide. It includes coverage of 34 million businesses worldwide and over 75 million executives worldwide. Companies can be located by name, ticker symbol, geographic location, SIC code, or company size.

Information provided by the Dun & Bradstreet <u>Million Dollar Directory</u> includes:

Number of employees
Address and phone numbers
Primary and secondary SIC
Ticker symbol
Location of incorporation if public
Names, titles, and short biographies of executives
Results can also be sorted by sales or geographic location

National Automobile Dealer Association (NADA)
NADA publishes several market reports on values of used vehicles. These reports are sold individually and are available at some libraries.

⌘   ⌘   ⌘   ⌘   ⌘

SPECIALIZED AUCTION COMPANIES

Some government agencies hire private contractors to sell their surplus property. Contact the contractor to be placed on their mailing list.

U.S. CUSTOMS SERVICE
EG&G Services
703-361-3131

DEPARTMENT OF DEFENSE
Government Liquidation, LLC
15051 N. Kierland Blvd., 3rd Floor
Scottsdale, AZ 85254
480-367-1300
www.govliquidation.com

GENERAL SERVICES ADMINISTRATION

Nationwide Auctions

Atlanta, GA	Chicago, IL
(404) 627-5346	(773) 287-4866
Industry, CA	Pico Rivera, CA
(626) 968-3110	(562) 463-6348
Benicia, CA	Ontario, CA
(707) 745-0119	(909) 605=8830

Kansas City, MO   St. Louis, MO
(816) 861-7079   (314) 389-3733

U.S. MARSHALS SERVICE

National Contractors:
Aircraft: Aero Mod Service Inc., Midland, TX
(915) 563-1666   www.aeromodservices.com

Real Estate: Fidelity Nat'l Asset Mgmt. Solutions,
Westminster, CO 80234 (800) 430-3320

Jewelry, Collectibles, Collector Coins, Art/Antiques:
Lone Star Auctioneers, Inc.
(817) 740-9400 or (800) 275-3336
www.lonestarauctioneers.com

Internet Sales:

On-Line Sales of Property:
Bid4assets   www.bid4assets.com
General Services Admin. (GSA) www.gsaauctions.gov

For state listings, call individual auction houses and ask
them who sells for government agencies. Usually you just
need to call one (call the largest auction house in your
area) and they will be able to tell you who conducts
government surplus auctions.

⌘　⌘　⌘　⌘　⌘

PARTICIPATING AGENCIES/BUSINESSES

Following is a list of agencies and businesses that conduct auctions or sales of surplus real and personal property. Many other agencies sell their property through the ones listed below (i.e.EG&G Technical Services sells items for U.S. Customs, the IRS, Secret Service, Bureau of Alcohol, Tobacco and Firearms, and the Food and Drug Administration.

- Banks
- U.S. Bankruptcy (USBK)
- Bureau of Land Management (BLM)
- Cooperative Administrative Support Units (CASU)
- U.S. Customs (USC)
- Department of Defense (DoD)
- Department of Transportation (DoT)
- Federal Deposit Insurance Corporation (FDIC)
- Federal Reserve Bank (FRB)
- General Services Administration (GSA)
- Internal Revenue Service (IRS)
- U.S. Marshal Sales (USMS)
- U.S. Post Office (USPS)
- Small Business Administration (SBA)

The following is included for each agency:

- General Information
- Sales Information
- Type of Sales
- Payment/Removal/Conditions
- Address(es)/Phone number(s)

⌘ ⌘ ⌘ ⌘ ⌘

PROPERTY FOR SALE

Below is a sampling of property sold by each agency.

Aircraft - DoD, IRS, USBK, USC, USMS, GSA

Antiques - Banks, IRS, USC, USBK, USMS

Art - IRS, USBK, USMS

Athletic Equipment - USBK, GSA, Local

Bicycles - USBK, GSA, Local

Boats/Marine - DoD, DoT, GSA, IRS, USC, USMS

Books - DoD, Local, USPS

Business Inventories - IRS, SBA

Camera Equipment - IRS, Local, USC, USBK

Collectibles - Banks, Local, USC, USMS

Clothing - DoD, USC, USPS

Computers - CASU, DoD, GSA, Local, SBA, USC, USMS, USPS

Construction Equipment - DoT, GSA, Police, USBK, USC

Electronics - CASU, DoD, Police, USC, USMS, USPS

Fitness Equipment - USBK, Police,

Fixtures - FDIC, USBK

Furniture - CASU, DoD, FDIC, GSA, IRS, Police, SBA, USC

Hardware - DoD, GSA

Housewares - DoD, USC, USPS

Jewelry - Banks, USC, USMS, USPS

Loans - FDIC

Machinery - DoD, DoT

Medical Equipment - DoD, GSA, USC

Metals/Recyclable Materials - DoD, DoT

Office Equipment/Supplies-CASU, DoD, GSA, USBK, SBA

Plumbing Equipment - DoD, USC

Real Estate-BLM, FDIC, GSA, IRS, SBA, USC, USMS

Restaurant Equipment - DoD, USBK

Stereo Equipment/CDs - USC, USPS

Treasury Bills, Notes, Bonds - FRB

Vehicles - DoD, DoT, GSA, Police, USC, USMS, USBK

Video Equipment - DoD, USBK, USPS

Wine, Liquor - DoT, USC

Agency Acronym Key

DoD - Department of Defense

DoT - Department of Transportation

FDIC - Federal Deposit Insurance Corporation

FRB - Federal Reserve Bank

GSA - General Services Administration

IRS - Internal Revenue Service

USBK - U.S. Bankruptcy

USC - U.S. Customs Service

USMS - U.S. Marshals Service

USPS - U.S. Post Office

⌘　⌘　⌘　⌘　⌘

U.S. BANKRUPTCY

General Information

By March 31, 2003, the number of personal and business bankruptcies numbered 1,611,268. The number of bankruptcies is on the rise. And that translates into more personal and real property available to be purchased through bankruptcy auctions.

Sales Information

One of the easiest ways to locate bankruptcy auctions is through the National Association of Bankruptcy Trustees. Their address follows:

One Windsor Cove, Suite 305
Columbia, SC 29223
(803) 252-5646

(800) 445-8629

On the Internet, go to **www.nabt.com**

Trustees handle various assets that are eventually sold after notice has been given to all creditors. <u>They are not required to provide notice of bankruptcy sales to the general public</u>. For sales of business property, the Trustee will usually appoint an auctioneer, who typically provides notice to the general public. They usually sell real property at a bankruptcy court sanctioned sale or they may hire a real estate broker to market the property. When a potential bid is accepted by the Trustee, he will provide notice of the sale through the Bankruptcy Court for a specific hearing date. The Judge will ask for other competitive bidders and will sell the property to the highest bidder. However, some Trustees sell property at sales held in their offices once notice has been served on the creditors and/or estate.

To obtain the location and dates of the auctions, the U.S. Trustee's Regional Office provides lists of U.S. Trustees in that region. Most Trustees hire professional auctioneers to conduct the sales. Request the auctioneer names from the Trustees, contact the auction companies and request to be placed on their mailing list. Because they often use specialized lists, **specify the type of property you are interested in purchasing.**

Another agent who may be involved is a Revenue Officer working for the IRS. This person steps in when non-payment of taxes is involved. If the seized property is to be sold at public sale under sealed bids, Form 2434–A, Notice of Sealed Bid Sale, details regarding this sale will be sent to you on this form. This lists:

Date/time bids will be opened
Place of sale/Inspection address
Title offered
Description of property
Submission of bids
Payment terms

Contact your local office for information about the property for sale. All bids must be submitted on Form 2222, "Sealed Bid for Purchase of Seized Property".

Payment/Removal/Conditions

All payments must be made by cash, certified, cashier's or treasurer's check or U.S. postal, bank, express or telegraph money order made payable to the IRS. Bids must be accompanied by the full amount of the bid if it totals $200 or less. If the total bid is more than $200, submit 20 percent of the amount bid or $200, whichever is *greater*.

U.S. Bankruptcy Trustees

To locate bankruptcy sales and auctions, call the closest regional office closest and request a list of individual trustees for that area. Contact them to receive details on upcoming sales and auctions.

⌘　⌘　⌘　⌘　⌘

BUREAU OF LAND MANAGEMENT

General Information

The Bureau of Land Management (BLM) is responsible for managing 262 million acres of land--about one-eighth of the land in the United States--and about 300 million additional acres of subsurface mineral resources.

Lands earmarked as excess to the public's and government's needs or more suited to private ownership are sometimes offered for sale. However, the BLM does not offer much land for sale because of a congressional mandate in 1976 to strive to retain these lands in public ownership.

Some local governments sell private land on which taxes have been delinquent to satisfy the tax debt. The Federal Government has no involvement in these sales. The best source for information is the **local county tax assessor** in the area involved.

There are two major categories of property which are available for sale: real property and public lands.

Real Property is primarily developed land with buildings, usually acquired by the Federal Government for a specific purpose such as a military base or office building. The GSA is the agency responsible for selling developed surplus property. (See GSA on Page **)

Public Land is undeveloped land with no improvements, usually part of the original public domain established during the western expansion of the United States. The BLM has the responsibility of selling this property.

Almost all of the property available is located in the states of Arizona, California, Colorado, Idaho, Montana, Nevada, New Mexico, Oregon, Utah, and Wyoming. *(Note: Because of land entitlements to the State of Alaska and to Alaska Natives, no public land sales will be conducted in Alaska in the foreseeable future.)*

There are small amounts in Alabama, Arkansas, Florida, Illinois, Kansas, Louisiana, Michigan, Minnesota, Missouri, Mississippi, Nebraska, North Dakota, Ohio, Oklahoma, South Dakota, Washington, and Wisconsin.

There are no public lands managed by the BLM in Connecticut, Delaware, Georgia, Hawaii, Indiana, Iowa, Kentucky, Maine, Maryland, Massachusetts, New Hampshire, New Jersey, New York, North Carolina, Pennsylvania, Rhode Island, South Carolina, Tennessee, Texas, Vermont, Virginia, and West Virginia.

Through its land-use planning process, the BLM identifies parcels of land for potential sale that fall into one of the following categories:

*scattered and isolated tracts that are difficult or uneconomical to manage;

*tracts acquired by the BLM for a specific purpose that are no longer needed; or

*land where disposal will serve important public objectives, such as community expansion and economic development.

Type of Sales

The BLM has three options for selling land:

modified competitive bidding where some preferences to adjoining landowners are recognized; direct sale to one party where circumstances warrant competitive bidding at public auction.

The sale method is determined on a case-by-case basis, depending on the circumstances of each particular parcel or sale. Sales are conducted by oral bid, sealed bid, or a combination of both.

Payment/Removal/Conditions

BLM can sell public land only to U.S. citizens or corporations subject to Federal or state laws.

Sale details are outlined in the sale notice from the BLM. A minimum percentage of the purchase price is required with each bid. If you are the successful bidder, the balance must be paid in full within a set period of time before a deed can be issued.

Long-term financing must be arranged through private lenders. The sale notice will clearly specify any Federal reservations or conditions of sale. **Make sure you have access to your property before buying** - check for roads or easements.

Check with the city or county involved to see if services as water, power and sewer services are available. Once you receive title, the land is subject to applicable state and local taxes, zoning ordinances, and other fees.

More detailed information, such as land reports and environmental assessments, is also available upon request for a copy fee.

⌘ ⌘ ⌘ ⌘ ⌘

U.S. CUSTOMS

General Information

The U.S. Customs agency sells property seized due to various reasons such as trademark or copyright violations, smuggling, drug trafficking, money laundering, credit card, mail or food stamp fraud, or other illegal activity. Either property was abandoned at ports of entry or duties were not paid. If goods are not claimed and entry not filed within 15 days, the goods will be held for six months and then sold at public auction.

U.S. Customs is now part of U.S. Customs and Border Protection (CBP). CBP sells merchandise abandoned or unclaimed at ports of entry by importers.

Live auctions are held in Long Beach, Calif. and Carteret, N.J. four times a year. Online auctions are available six times per year.

Sales Information

This website is a great source for general merchandise:

http://www.cwsmarketing.com

For vehicles less than $10,000, visit:

http://www.robertsonauto.com

For vehicles valued greater than $10,000, visit:

https://www.treasury.gov/auctions/treasury/gp

Updates can be subscribed to by visiting the site:
https://help.cbp.gov/app/answers/detail/a_id/265/~ /auction-schedules

On the lefthand side of the page, click on "Subscribe to Updates."

⌘　⌘　⌘　⌘　⌘

DEPARTMENT OF DEFENSE

General Information

The Department of Defense disposes of excess property received from the military services. The main entity used to dispose of this property is the Defense Logistics Agency. DLA inventories, evaluates and revalues reusable military resources. Property remaining after all attempts to re-use it in other agencies have been attempted, it is sold to the public in order to generate operating revenues.

Property disposed of by the DLA Disposition Services changes daily and includes thousands of items from air conditioners, clothing, computers, vehicles and much more. Offensive and defensive military <u>weapons are sold only as scrap</u>; they are rendered useless through the demilitarization process.

Sales Information

DLA Disposition Services has a searchable database that makes it easy to find the property. The inventory is updated nightly and contains over 600,000 items. The government identifies items by assignment of a National

Stock Number (NSN). Numbers are assigned based on the end use of the item. The NSN is a 13-digit number. (for example, 6645-00-123-3568).

A quick way to access property information is via **property search area** on the Internet. The entire DRMS inventory is available for search. Property can be searched by FSC (Federal Supply Code), NSN (National Stock Number) or by Item Name. Descriptions can be viewed via the Defense Logistics Agency:

www.sales.dla.mil/dlab2b/init.do

Find a step-by-step guide on how to purchase from the DLA here:

http://www.dla.mil/DispositionServices/Business/Findand
AcquireItems.aspx

Payment/Removal/Conditions

Letter of Acceptance

Digitized LOA/electronic signatures and submission must be on file prior to removal of awarded property from any location.

DLA Customer Service: For all other or general questions:
1-877-DLA-CALL (1-877-352-2255)

or send an email to DLAContactCenter@dla.mil

⌘   ⌘   ⌘   ⌘   ⌘

DEPARTMENT OF TRANSPORTATION

General Information

The Department of Transportation was established by an act of Congress on October 15, 1966.

Sales Information

The Federal DOT supplies money to individual states for use in building and maintaining its roads. Therefore, the states own the vehicles and equipment. The only highways the Federal government takes care of are on the property owned by the Forest Service, Park Service and Bureau of Indian Affairs. Vehicles such as 4-wheel drives and trucks are purchased from the GSA and when the Federal government is through with them, the vehicles are *returned to the GSA and are sold by them.* Basically, the Federal agency has little or no equipment of its own to sell and does not hold auctions.

However, some state agencies do hold auctions selling real estate and other surplus property. *By Federal law they must advertise the auctions in local newspapers.*

Type of Sale

Public auction, sealed bid and direct sale are the types of sales employed most often by this agency.

Payment/Removal/Conditions

Full payment is required at the time of the sale. Payment can take the form of cash and personal or business checks, but checks must be accompanied by a bank letter guaranteeing payment. No credit cards are accepted. Nothing shall be removed from the auction site until payment is made in full. The DOT is not responsible for any vehicles or other property after the sale.

All items will be sold on an "As Is and Where Is" basis. The DOT makes no guarantees, warranties or representation, expressed or implied, written or oral, as to the condition of vehicles or miscellaneous items, or their fitness for any purpose or the quantity for sale.

To locate the Department of Transportation for your state, check the government pages in your phone book.

⌘ ⌘ ⌘ ⌘ ⌘

FEDERAL DEPOSIT INSURANCE CORPORATION

General Information

The Federal Deposit Insurance Corporation (FDIC), created in 1933, insures deposits in banks and thrift institutions for up to $100,000. It was created in response to the 1000's of bank failures that occurred in the 1920s and early 1930s.

The FDIC sells residential, commercial and land assets and loans that it has acquired through bank failures.

Sale Information

All sales and auctions conducted on behalf of the FDIC can be found on-line at:

https://www.fdic.gov/

Sales calendar for all sales here:

https://www.fdic.gov/buying/calendar/event-calendar.html

For specific types of property, using the following:

Real Estate
http://www.fdicrealestatelistings.com/

Loan Sales
https://www.fdic.gov/buying/loan/announcements.html

"Loan sale" is a common term for sale of loans or loan pools. (Loans grouped by loan size, quality, type, etc.) Loans acquired by the FDIC from failed financial institutions are generally sold in pools through sealed bid sale or English outcry auction. (See Glossary)

The FDIC does not guarantee the performance of loans being sold. All loans are sold with limited, if any, representations and warranties.

Financial Assets
https://www.fdic.gov/buying/financial/qualification_process.html

The assets include small dollar/geographically focused

loan pools in structured transactions

Assets from Failed Banks

https://www.fdic.gov/buying/otherasset/failedbank/index.html

Inventory includes furniture, fixtures and equipment.

Past Sales Records

https://www.fdic.gov/buying/historical/index.html

Once you have found a property you are interested in, get in touch with the individual listed as the "Contact" in the information you receive regarding the property. The contact will either be an individual from an FDIC office or someone associated with the sales process (e.g. auction company, real estate broker). If a Property Information Package ("PIP") has been prepared on a particular property, it can be obtained from this individual. The property listings are updated by the close of business each Monday, so check weekly to determine if a property is still available.

KEEP IN MIND: As with most auctioned property, property is sold in an "AS IS" condition.

For further help, call the FDIC Call Center:

Toll-free numbers:
- 877-ASKFDIC (877-275-3342)
- TDD: 800-925-4618

To get on the FDIC Asset Marketing e-mail list, register at:

**https://service.govdelivery.com/accounts/USFDIC/
subscriber/new**

⌘ ⌘ ⌘ ⌘ ⌘

GENERAL SERVICES ADMINISTRATION

General Information

One of the functions of the General Services Administration (GSA) is to disposes of personal property (furniture, computers, equipment, vehicles, etc.). If property cannot be used (or is not wanted) by another federal agency, it is declared surplus.

(800) 488-3111

The GSA first offers the property to the State Agencies for Surplus Property (SASP) for donation. Non-federal entities (public and private agencies, non-profit organizations and institutions, and programs for the elderly and homeless) can obtain surplus federal personal property through the SASP.

Sales Information

In general, the GSA does not maintain a mailing list for property disposal. However, sales are advertised in local and national newspapers, in trade publications, on the radio and signs are placed on the property. Additionally, the GSA sells property using Internet auction, live auction, sealed bid, fixed price, spot bid, and negotiated sales. GSA Auctions® is an on-line system used to place bids electronically. The website address is:

https://gsaauctions.gov/gsaauctions/gsaauctions/

Sales information is advertised through mailing lists for **frequent purchasers**, radio, television or newspaper announcements, trade journals and periodicals, and notices in town halls, post offices, and Federal Government buildings.

Sales of national interest are published in the Commerce Business Daily. Copies may be available at libraries and local Chambers of Commerce. For subscription information to the Commerce Business Daily, call the U.S. Government Printing Office at (866) 512-1800 or write:

Superintendent of Documents

U.S. Government Printing Office

Washington, D.C. 20402

Names of people who don't buy are periodically removed from the list. *To be placed on the mailing list, write to the*

GSA sales office serving your location.

The GSA also sells real property no longer needed by the government. Property is sold in all 50 states, District of Columbia, Puerto Rico, Virgin Islands, and U.S. Pacific territories. To receive a booklet with an explanation of the GSA sales program and a list of all properties for sale, call the GSA Office of Property Disposal and leave your name, phone and address.

(800) 472-1313

The GSA website for real property is:

http://propertydisposal.gsa.gov/property/

Another option is to request a copy of *U.S. Real Property Sales List* from:

Consumer Information Center
Department 514A
Pueblo, CO 81009

Ads are also run in local newspapers and on radio. Specialized sales and others that might generate interest nationwide are advertised in national newspapers, trade journals and periodicals.

Vehicle Auctions

GSA Fleet will sell approximately 35,000 vehicles this

coming year. Most vehicles will be available between April–September, when a majority of the leases expire.

For information on sales, call your nearest Fleet Management Center (**FMC**) under the GSA listing in the phone book.

For GSA Fleet Vehicle Sales, go to:

http://www.autoauctions.gsa.gov/

Type of Sale

GSA conducts sealed bid, fixed price, auction, spot bid, or negotiated sales. It is GSA policy to sell personal property at fair market value, and not to sell items if the bid price is below what is reasonable.

Payment/Removal/Conditions

Acceptable forms of payment generally include cash, cashier's check, money orders, traveler's checks, credit cards (Visa, MasterCard, Discover, Bravo and Private Issue), government checks and credit union checks (checks issued by Federal or State chartered credit unions - no share draft/checking account checks.) Personal or Company/Business checks are not acceptable unless accompanied by an informal bank letter guaranteeing payment. Failure of the Credit Card bank to grant approval for the amount of purchase **does not void the contract**. The purchaser is still responsible for payment in accordance with the Terms and Conditions of the sale.

The successful bidder *must make all removal arrangements*, including packing, crating, removal and transportation. The Property Custodian must be notified in writing of such arrangements and have proper authorization to release property to anyone other than the successful bidder. They will not make any removal arrangements. If you fail to pay and remove by the deadline, the government is entitled to retain/collect 20% of total bid price.

For information on GSA sales of used federal personal property, or to be placed on a mailing list, write to Personal Property Sales, U.S. General Services Administration, at the address below serving your location. For information about upcoming sales, you may call the telephone number listed with each address or visit www.gsa.gov.

⌘　⌘　⌘　⌘　⌘

INTERNAL REVENUE SERVICE

General Information

Under the Internal Revenue Code, the Internal Revenues Services has the authority to seize or otherwise acquire property from people for nonpayment of taxes or for illegal acts such as sale of drugs, tax fraud and criminal activities.

Sales Information

The IRS does not maintain a mailing list for sales. However, the U.S. Customs Service Support offers a subscription program for people interested in receiving sales flyers on personal property. To subscribe, go to:

https://help.cbp.gov/app/answers/detail/a_id/265/~/auction-schedules

For upcoming sales, visit their website:

https://www.treasury.gov/auctions/irs/index.html

A wide variety of items are sold including antiques, art, jewelry, collectible, automobiles, motorcycles, real estate, financial instruments, patents, royalties, household goods.

The following sites hold auctions:

EG&G Services/CWS Marketing auctions (general merchandise)

Rod Robertson Enterprises (vehicles valued less than $10,000)

VSE Warehouse (vehicles valued greater than $10,000)

Customs and Border Protection (CBP) sells merchandise abandoned or unclaimed at ports of entry by public auction. Live auctions are held in Long Beach, Calif. and Carteret, N.J. four times a year. Online auctions are available six times per year.

Type of Sale

There are two types of sales used to sell IRS property: 1) Public Auction and 2) Sealed Bid Auction. Both of these are open to the public. The auctioneer is usually a Property and Liquidation Specialist with the IRS. At the end of the auction, the property will be awarded to the highest bidder, contingent upon a review of records to make sure the winning bidder is not the violator or associated with the violator. Buyers will be notified within 72 hours of the auction date.

Potential bidders should request a copy of the Notice of Public Auction or Notice of Sealed Bid Auction and read it thoroughly for sale requirements.

Payment/Removal/Conditions

Payment for all property sold must be in the form of cash, certified check, cashier's check, or treasurer's check drawn on any bank or trust company incorporated under the laws of the U.S. or under the laws of any state or possession of the United States. A U.S. postal, bank, express, or money order and made out to the U.S. Treasury are also acceptable.

⌘　⌘　⌘　⌘　⌘

U.S. MARSHALS SERVICE

General Information

The U.S. Marshals Service (USMS) manages and sells assets seized from criminal enterprises, including illegal activities against the USMS, Dept. of Justice agencies (DEA, FBI, INS, and ATF), and certain other federal law enforcement agencies.

The USMS sells various types of property such as: residential and commercial real estate, vacant land, business establishments, financial instruments and a wide range of personal property such as motor vehicles, boats, aircraft, jewelry, art, antiques, and collectibles.

Sales Information

The USMS does not maintain a list of sale property or notify buyers of sales. However, they do use a National Sellers List which provides names and contact information for specific sellers of certain type of surplus property. It also includes state-by-state listings for sellers. For the

www.ingramcontent.com/pod-product-compliance
Lightning Source LLC
Chambersburg PA
CBHW060645290526
45793CB00001B/409

complete list, click on National Sellers List in the right hand column at:

https://www.usmarshals.gov/assets/

Current auctions being held can be found at:
https://www.usmarshals.gov/assets/index.html

Other ways to obtain information:

- Send your name, address and a check or money order for $1.50 to Federal Citizen Information Center, Dept. 319P, Pueblo, CO 81009.
- Call 1-888-878-3256, request Item 319V
- http://publications.usa.gov

Current auctions being held can be found at:
https://www.usmarshals.gov/assets/index.html

Type of Sales

Forfeited property is sold through a variety of methods including negotiation, sealed bid and auction.

Payment/Removal/Conditions

Guaranteed payment such as cash or certified check is required. Credit cards may be accepted at some of the sales.

Property must be sold for its fair market value. U.S. Marshals reserve the right to reject any bids in a sale. Department of Justice employees, certain contractors, and criminal defendants are prohibited from bidding.

Some areas have established a *forfeiture sales information line*. To obtain information, call the District Offices in your area.

https://www.usmarshals.gov/district/county.htm

⌘　⌘　⌘　⌘　⌘

U.S. POST OFFICE

General Information

As of September, the U.S. Post Office had handled 202,185 million pieces of mail in 2003. It stands to reason that some of the pieces would not make it to their destination due to various reasons. When this happens, the article is sent to one of three mail recovery centers. At these centers, every attempt is made to identify the sender or recipient. If the sender or recipient cannot be identified, the item is held for a period of time, then either disposed of or auctioned. (Note: Only two centers hold sales.)

The merchandise may include clocks, televisions, radios, tape recorders, jewelry, VCRs, and clothing. The USPS also has sales programs that sell excess postal vehicles, computers, workroom and office furniture, and electronic and hardware items for mail handling equipment.

Sales Information

Whereas in the past several post offices held auctions for

lost and undeliverable items, now all surplus property is now conducted online at:

https://www.govdeals.com/index.cfm?fa=Main.AdvSearch ResultsNew&agency=4703

Note: It has been determined that it is difficult - but not impossible - to find good deals at gov.deals. We caution buyers "caveat emptor."

⌘ ⌘ ⌘ ⌘ ⌘

STATE AGENCIES - SURPLUS PROPERTY

Federal surplus personal property programs enable the public to purchase property. Ask the agency representative for eligibility requirements.

Alabama	(334) 277-5866
Alaska	(907) 279-0596
American Samoa	(684) 699-1170
Arizona	(602) 542-5701
Arkansas	(501) 835-3111
California	(714) 449-5900
Colorado	(303) 370-2160
Connecticut	(860) 713-5086
Delaware	(302) 836-7640
District of Columbia	(202) 576-6472
Florida	(202) 576-6472
Georgia	(404)756-4801
Guam	(671) 472-1725
Hawaii	(808) 831-6757
Idaho	(208) 327-7471
Illinois	(217) 785-6903
Indiana	(317) 260-4200

Iowa	(515) 953-5747
Kansas	(785) 296-2351
Kentucky	(502) 564-4836
Louisiana	(225) 342-7860
Maine	(207) 287-2923
Maryland	(410) 540-4067
Massachusetts	(617) 720-3146
Michigan	(517) 335-9106
Minnesota	(651) 639-4023
Mississippi	(601) 939-2050
Missouri	(573) 751-3415
Montana	(406) 444-4514
Nebraska	(402) 471-2677
Nevada	(775) 688-1161
New Hampshire	(603) 271-3239
New Jersey	(609) 452-2601
New Mexico	(505) 476-1904
New York	(518) 457-3264
North Carolina	(919) 733-3885
North Dakota	(701) 328-9667
No. Mariana Islands	(670) 664-1500
Ohio	(614) 466-4485
Oklahoma	(405) 425-2700

Oregon	(503) 378-4711
Pennsylvania	(717) 787-9724
Puerto Rico	(787) 759-7676
Rhode Island	(401) 222-5801
South Carolina	(803) 896-6880
South Dakota	(605) 353-7150
Tennessee	(615) 350-3373
Texas	(512) 463-9709
Utah	(801) 619-7200
Vermont	(802) 828-3394
Virginia	(804) 236-3675
Virgin Islands	(340) 774-0828
Washington	(253) 333-4907
West Virginia	(304) 766-2626
Wisconsin	(608) 849-2449
Wyoming	(307) 777-7901

Other titles by Ellen L. Hughes

105 Ways to Make Money at Home

Adventures With Natural Healing - *A Health Junkie's Journey Through Alternative Medicine*

Be A Smart Client - *How To Hire The Best Lawyer and Help Win Your Case*

Dental Heaven - *Get A Great Smile Without Paying Through The Nose*

Government Auctions/Sales Manual

Home Office Handbook

Re-Energize Yourself - *Simple Techniques to Recharge Your Body and Mind*

* * *

Office Wizard - *A Personalized Office Procedures Manual (software)*

More to come…

www.themckeecompany.com